This beginning
belongs to you.

Start Today

COMPENDIUM®
live inspired.

WRITTEN BY M.H. CLARK ~ DESIGNED BY HEIDI RODRIGUEZ

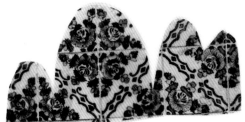

Today has a lot going for it:

It's here, it's now, and it's already yours.

Today is the only day that comes with a guarantee.

You've been waiting for today, even though you might have been calling it something else. You might have been calling it "tomorrow" or "someday" or even "the future." But now, it's the present, and the best thing to do with any present is open it, delight in it, and appreciate it for what it is.

Begin something—something small or something bold, something that will grow bigger with time. This might just be the day you've been waiting for. So start here, start now. Start today.

Deep.

Uncover the dream
you've been hiding like a pearl
and lift it to the surface.

Let it shine.

You can decide how
much distance
there will be between
the life you have

and the life you want.

This, right here,
is where your tomorrows
are built.

Even spring doesn't come all at once.

Spring comes
leaf by leaf.

Start here.

Start
Today.

Start slowly
if you need to go slowly.
Start with uncertainty,
start without a road map,
start without even knowing
when you will arrive.

But don't stop.

At a certain point,

it's no longer about what's already happened.

It's about what's going to happen.

It's about everything that's coming next.

There is
more risk in
waiting

than in
beginning.

It isn't that your heart
wants too much.

It's that your heart knows
    how much is possible.

Seize potential.

Start today.

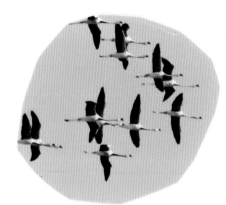

The sign you've been
waiting for doesn't always
come with bright lights
hanging over it.

Sometimes, it's more like
a quiet voice that sidles up
next to you and says,
"begin."

Get good at recognizing your dream.

Get so good that when it is arriving, you can see it coming and run to meet it.

Feed and water
your dream.

Walk it in the sun.
Give it a place where it can grow.

Go beyond
your

fear.

Give yourself this gift:

Start Today.

Turn your desire into
momentum.
Create something
better.

Small steps add up.

Keep wishing.
Keep walking.

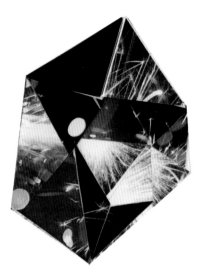

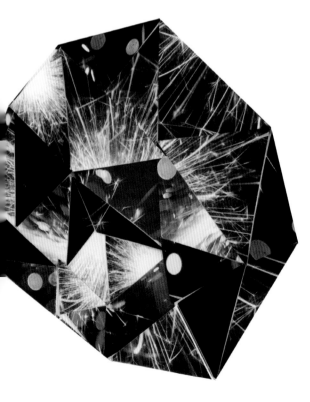

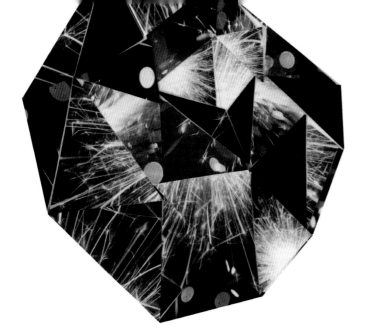
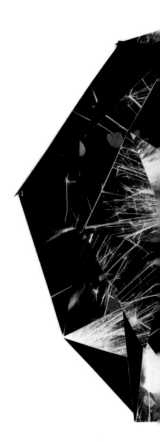

Make your dream become your life.
Do the thing you long to do.

When you begin doing
the thing you want to do,
the future isn't any
more predictable.

But you start to
look forward to it more.

Wonderful things
can take time.

Start
today.

Your life deserves a
wild chance.
A new direction.
A perfect, stunning
change for the best.

What better reason
than this:

you've always
     wanted to.

In order to begin,
you need only be as
strong, as capable,
as ready as you are
right now.

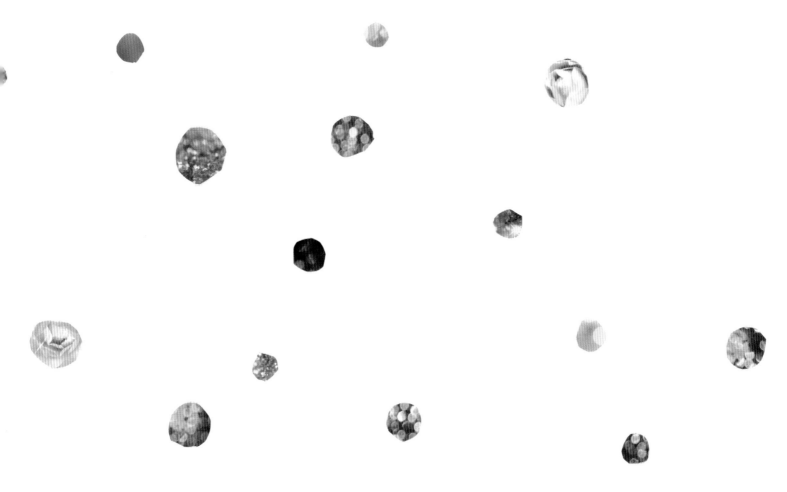

There are as many
opportunities
as there are moments
in each day.

But you don't get them all.
You only get the ones you
choose to take.

Make tomorrow happy.

Start Today.

It is completely possible
for one small
spark of action
on one completely
ordinary day to alter the
shape of everything
that follows.

It isn't impossible
if you have imagined it.
It isn't far if you
can see it.
It isn't unreachable if you
have begun.

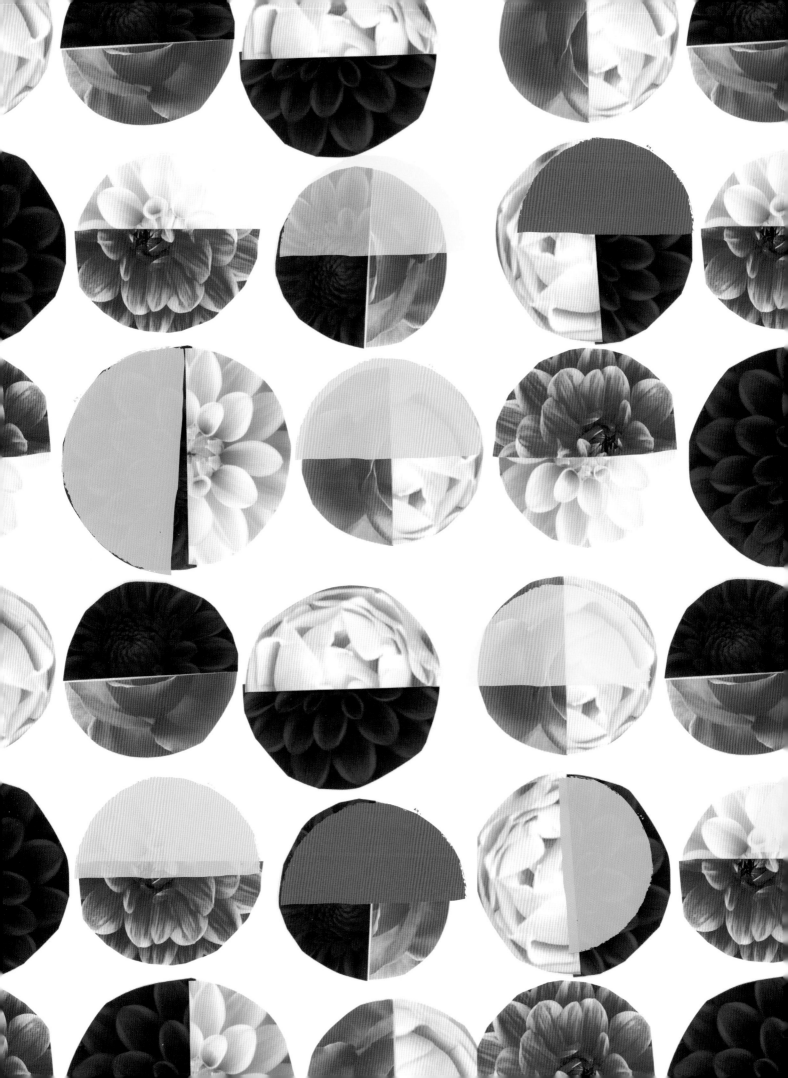

Do it for yourself.

Do it for the thing
you long for,
the thing you fall asleep
dreaming of, and
wake up wanting.

Choose a
moment in which
anything
can happen.

Why not this one?

Decide
to
start
today.

COMPENDIUM®
live inspired.

With special thanks to the entire Compendium family.

CREDITS:

WRITTEN BY: M.H. CLARK
DESIGNED BY: HEIDI RODRIGUEZ
EDITED BY: AMELIA RIEDLER
CREATIVE DIRECTION BY: JULIE FLAHIFF

PHOTOGRAPHY CREDITS:

AKAI / PHOTOCASE.COM: PAGE 58; HEAVYHAWK / PHOTOCASE.COM: PAGES 24-25; TOSINI / PHOTOCASE.COM: PAGES 20, 40-41, 59; STEKO7 / PHOTOCASE.COM: PAGES 8, 21; MAIWIND / PHOTOCASE.COM: PAGES 17, 28-29, 44, 49; SE.W / PHOTOCASE.COM: PAGE 21; FRÄULEIN.PALINDROM / PHOTOCASE.COM: PAGE 8; SKYLA80 / PHOTOCASE.COM: PAGE 44; SICKRICK / PHOTOCASE.COM: PAGE 21; JOEXX / PHOTOCASE.COM: PAGE 21; SUZE / PHOTOCASE.COM: PAGES 24-25; PIXELNEST / PHOTOCASE.COM: PAGE 25; PENCAKE / PHOTOCASE.COM: PAGES 17, 28-29, 44, 49; OVOKURO / PHOTOCASE.COM: PAGES 24-25; LUMAMARIN / PHOTOCASE.COM: PAGES 4, 8, 18-19; EISENGLIMMER / PHOTOCASE.COM: PAGES 4, 18-19, 21; IRINA / PHOTOCASE.COM: PAGE 4; LUCELUCELUCEIMAGES / VEER.COM: PAGES 50-51, 58; MINDSTORM / VEER.COM: PAGE 44; STEPHANIE FREY / VEER.COM: PAGES 50-51; DENIS DRYASHKIN / VEER.COM: PAGES 50-51, 58; HOMYDESIGN / VEER.COM: PAGES 2, 40-41; STOCKSNAPPER / VEER.COM: PAGES 38-39, 54-55; SALLY WALLIS / ISTOCK / THINKSTOCK: PAGES 10-11, 17, 28-29, 35, 57; ADELE DE WITTE / ISTOCK / THINKSTOCK: PAGES 10-11, 35, 44, 57; JUPITERIMAGES / PHOTOS.COM / THINKSTOCK: PAGES 10-11, 17, 28-29, 35, 44, 49, 57; UDO FEINWEBER / ISTOCK / THINKSTOCK: PAGES 35, 44, 57; SDANNAS / ISTOCK / THINKSTOCK: PAGES 10-11, 35, 44, 57.

Library of Congress Control Number: 2013957287

ISBN: 978-1-938298-26-4

1st printing. Printed in China with soy inks.